The Urbana Free Library

To renew: call 217-367-4057
or go to "*urbanafreelibrary.org*"
and select "Renew/Request Items"

SNAKES ALIVE

Adders

by Ellen Frazel

BELLWETHER MEDIA • MINNEAPOLIS, MN

4·12
22⁰⁰

Note to Librarians, Teachers, and Parents:

Blastoff! Readers are carefully developed by literacy experts and combine standards-based content with developmentally appropriate text.

Level 1 provides the most support through repetition of high-frequency words, light text, predictable sentence patterns, and strong visual support.

Level 2 offers early readers a bit more challenge through varied simple sentences, increased text load, and less repetition of high-frequency words.

Level 3 advances early-fluent readers toward fluency through increased text and concept load, less reliance on visuals, longer sentences, and more literary language.

Level 4 builds reading stamina by providing more text per page, increased use of punctuation, greater variation in sentence patterns, and increasingly challenging vocabulary.

Level 5 encourages children to move from "learning to read" to "reading to learn" by providing even more text, varied writing styles, and less familiar topics.

Whichever book is right for your reader, Blastoff! Readers are the perfect books to build confidence and encourage a love of reading that will last a lifetime!

This edition first published in 2012 by Bellwether Media, Inc.

No part of this publication may be reproduced in whole or in part without written permission of the publisher. For information regarding permission, write to Bellwether Media, Inc., Attention: Permissions Department, 5357 Penn Avenue South, Minneapolis, MN 55419.

Library of Congress Cataloging-in-Publication Data

Frazel, Ellen.
  Adders / by Ellen Frazel.
    p. cm. – (Blastoff! Readers. Snakes alive)
  Includes bibliographical references and index.
  Summary: "Simple text and full-color photography introduce beginning readers to adders. Developed by literacy experts for students in kindergarten through third grade"–Provided by publisher.
  ISBN 978-1-60014-612-1 (hardcover : alk. paper)
  1. Vipera berus–Juvenile literature. I. Title.
  QL666.O69F73 2011
  597.96'36–dc22
                                    2011004207

Text copyright © 2012 by Bellwether Media, Inc. BLASTOFF! READERS and associated logos are trademarks and/or registered trademarks of Bellwether Media, Inc.

Printed in the United States of America, North Mankato, MN.

080111   1187

Contents

How Adders Look 4

Where Adders Live 10

Hunting and Feeding 14

Glossary 22

To Learn More 23

Index 24

Adders are small, **poisonous** snakes. They are the only snakes that can control how much **venom** they release.

Adders weigh up to 4 pounds (1.8 kilograms). They are between 12 and 36 inches (30 and 91 centimeters) long.

Adders can be light or dark in color. Females are usually brown or red. Males are often white, yellow, or gray.

Most adders
have dark zigzag
patterns on their
bodies. Many have
a mark on their
head that looks like
a "V" or an "X."

scutes

Adders have **scales** that cover and protect their bodies. The scales on their bellies are called **scutes**.

Strong muscles pull on the scutes to help adders move forward. Adders **shed** their skin when it gets too tight.

= areas where adders live

Adders can be found from western Europe to eastern Asia. They are the only snakes that live in the **Arctic Circle**.

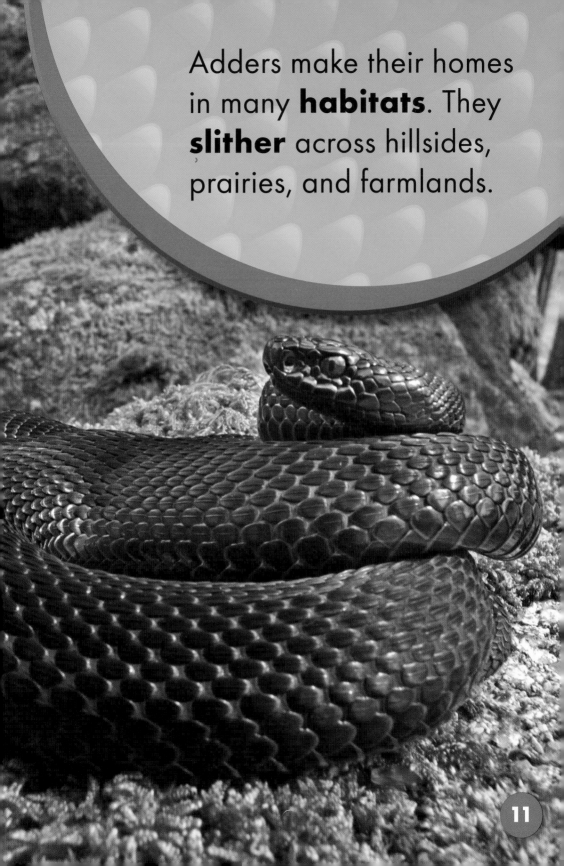

Adders make their homes in many **habitats**. They **slither** across hillsides, prairies, and farmlands.

Adders **hibernate** in the winter. They stay warm under logs or in empty **burrows**.

In spring, adders come out of hibernation. They **bask** under the sun to warm their bodies.

Adders hunt for food at night.
The markings on their bodies
help them hide while they
watch for **prey**.

They stay still and wait for mice, frogs, and birds. They also eat spiders, weasels, and small lizards.

adder prey

fangs

An adder **strikes** when prey comes near. It sinks its **fangs** into the animal.

Venom moves through its hollow fangs and into the prey. Then it lets the prey go.

The adder does not fight with the prey. It waits for its venom to spread through the animal.

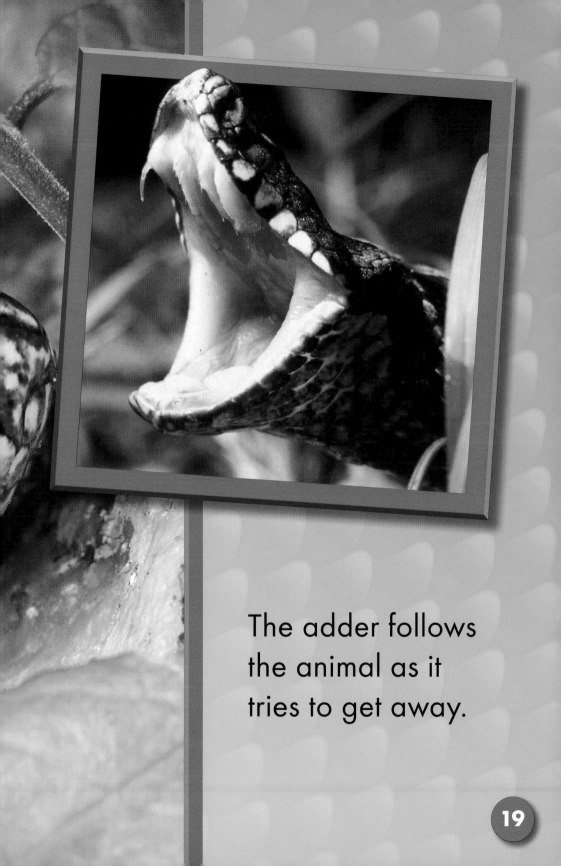

The adder follows
the animal as it
tries to get away.

Soon the prey is dead
or unable to move.

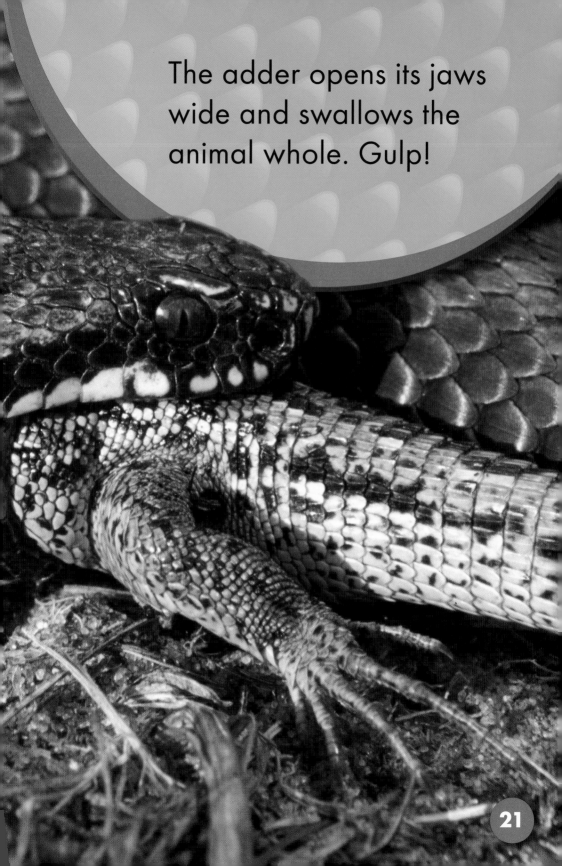

The adder opens its jaws wide and swallows the animal whole. Gulp!

Glossary

Arctic Circle—Earth's northernmost region; the Arctic Circle includes the North Pole.

bask—to soak up heat from the sun or another source of light

burrows—holes or tunnels in the ground made by animals

fangs—sharp, curved teeth; adders have hollow fangs through which venom can move into a bite.

habitats—environments in which a plant or animal usually lives

hibernate—to be inactive during winter

poisonous—able to kill or harm with a poison; the venom adders make is a poison.

prey—an animal hunted by another animal for food

scales—small plates of skin that cover and protect a snake's body

scutes—large scales on the belly of a snake that are attached to muscles; snakes use scutes to move from place to place.

shed—to let something fall off

slither—to slide

strikes—quickly throws the head and front part of the body at a predator or prey

venom—a poison that some snakes make; adder venom is deadly.

To Learn More

AT THE LIBRARY

Gibbons, Gail. *Snakes*. New York, N.Y.: Holiday House, 2007.

Klein, Adam G. *Common Adders*. Edina, Minn.: Abdo Pub., 2006.

Whittley, Sarah. *Snakes*. New York, N.Y.: St. Martin's Press, 2002.

ON THE WEB

Learning more about adders is as easy as 1, 2, 3.

1. Go to www.factsurfer.com.

2. Enter "adders" into the search box.

3. Click the "Surf" button and you will see a list of related Web sites.

With factsurfer.com, finding more information is just a click away.

Index

Arctic Circle, 10
Asia, 10
basking, 13
burrows, 12
colors, 6
Europe, 10
fangs, 16, 17
farmlands, 11
habitats, 11
hibernation, 12, 13
hillsides, 11
hunting, 14
jaws, 21
length, 5
markings, 7, 14
patterns, 7
poisonous, 4
prairies, 11
prey, 14, 15, 16, 17, 18, 20

scales, 8
scutes, 8, 9
shedding, 9
slithering, 11
spring, 13
striking, 16
swallowing, 21
venom, 4, 17, 18
weight, 5
winter, 12

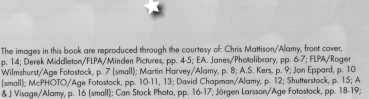

The images in this book are reproduced through the courtesy of: Chris Mattison/Alamy, front cover, p. 14; Derek Middleton/FLPA/Minden Pictures, pp. 4-5; EA. Janes/Photolibrary, pp. 6-7; FLPA/Roger Wilmshurst/Age Fotostock, p. 7 (small); Martin Harvey/Alamy, p. 8; A.S. Kers, p. 9; Jon Eppard, p. 10 (small); McPHOTO/Age Fotostock, pp. 10-11, 13; David Chapman/Alamy, p. 12; Shutterstock, p. 15; A & J Visage/Alamy, p. 16 (small); Can Stock Photo, pp. 16-17; Jörgen Larsson/Age Fotostock, pp. 18-19; blickwinkel/Alamy, p. 19 (small); Artur Tabor/naturepl.com, p. 21.